Franchise Operations Manual

- inexpensive operation
- ease of duplication
- detailed systems, processes and procedures
- a new idea, a different approach
- pops up anywhere
- easy to do

IDI GROUP
CONSUMER RESEARCH

BIG BUSINESS SERVICES
LOCAL APPROACH

QUALITY MARKET RESEARCH, QUICK AND COST-
EFFECTIVE

↑

This was everything anybody needs to know about IDI Group.
What follows is everything you need to know about IDI Group.

By Mr. X and Mr. Z

"I started with the resources of a lemonade stand."

I'm a smart kid who couldn't get it together. My friend and I can't make IDI Group national. You can.

Information is our strongest commodity. People always need information, and people always need more information.

Information is a renewable resource. We harvest information, we refine that information, and then we package it to sell.

These are my notes, sales materials, action plans, scripts, surveys, philosophy and analysis. Emails, rough notes, dead ends. Start to finish. Everything you need to know to start and succeed with IDI is in this manual. Simply consult the manual.

X and Z share over twenty years of management experience in the fields of finance, sales, marketing and publications.

As a team, they have worked side by side for the past 3 years, sharing their expertise with a local approach that has a global destination.

Pretend I left my briefcase at the restaurant, and before you could run after me, I was gone! It's a bit of a mess, but you are welcome to look inside!

IMMEDIATE RELEASE
Anytown, USA

My name is X. My best friend, Z, and I started the IDI Group under the umbrella of a local ad agency.

We provide advertising research to assist locally owned businesses communicate their messages more effectively. The two of us developed methods that can provide a business with better information, that is quick and extremely cost effective. We realized that there is more valuable data within conversations with people, than you get asking the same stock questions. Our motto is that, "A conversation is the best way to learn. Have enough conversations and you will have an education."

We are proud to provide a research service that has been previously unavailable on the scale of local business. We take the lead with an approach that combines the latest technology with friendly faces. We transcribe speech to text for quality control, but more importantly, we ask open questions, listen attentively, and objectively pass that feedback on to businesses.

We started with nothing more than an idea. Information is a free, renewable resource. You just have to tap into it. We harvest information from people in the community, we refine that information, and we package that information in a way that business leaders can easily access and share. You could say, we spin conversations into gold!

We have a local approach with a global appeal. We hope that you can see some value in the information we provide. What we have learned, is that a conversation, like a good story, always has a value- it can hold the public's attention for a lifetime.

Thank you,

X, Z

QUALITY RESEARCH, QUICK AND COST EFFECTIVE
Manual
Table of Contents

1. Welcome to IDI
2. How to use this Manual
3. IDI FAQs
4. Your in-home Focus Group
5. In-home materials
6. Sending the data and getting paid

Sales Materials
1. IDI Overview of Services
2. IDI Difference
3. IDI Data Collection
4. IDI Analysis
5. IDI History
6. IDI Headquarters
7. IDI Team

Training
1. Getting certified
2. your secure log-in
3. Qualities of success

Education Materials
1. Opinions and Observations

Press and Media
1. Press release templates

Survey Materials

About the storyboard

Welcome to the IDI Group!

This manual provides quick answers and step-by-step solutions to get you going and keep you going straight to the top with us!

IDI Group provides American businesses with the consumer data they need to meet and exceed the expectations of the consumer. Your experience puts you right in the center of national media and communications.

IDI Group takes the valuable feedback you gather at each in-home Focus Group, and provides the business community with key information to make informed business decisions.

Thank you in advance,

-X, Z

Manual

Business Overview

A Tupperware Party is the perfect environment to conduct market research. The only reason people may be reluctant to attend a Tupperware Party is that they feel obligated to buy something. These in-home Focus Groups have zero sales involved. In fact each guest leaves with incentives!

We developed a workbook to lead the in-home consultant through the one hour Focus Group. The workbook looks like your favorite magazine. Glossy advertisements, fun facts, pop quizzes... Each section the guest completes will reveal something exciting about their personal consumer profile.

After the guests leave, the in home consultant enters each guest's consumer scores via a secure website, emails audio files for quality control, and mails completed workbooks to headquarters. The consultant is paid a flat fee, direct deposit, for each completed workbook.

Headquarters compiles all information into a database, and sells chunks of data to businesses. Head quarters completes larger projects to gain exposure and credibility.

IDI GROUP

Your first In-home Focus Group

By now you should be expecting 10-12 guests in about an hour. If your guest list is not what you expected, refer the corresponding chapter.

Please make sure that you have a IDI Group Storyboard for each expected guests. If you anticipate that you will run short of storyboards in the next two weeks, please order more. See "Supplies" form.

Prepare light snacks. Make sure you have the incentive gifts.

Guests should begin arriving at 5:30 PM and you should be ready to go at 6PM.

Set digital audio recorder on record, to assure proper quality control.

Hand each guest their storyboard. Let the storyboard lead you step by step through the next one hour.

Assure each guest there there are absolutely no sales involved, there is no right or wrong answer, and all information is completely confidential. No one receives their contact info. They will not be contacted by anyone, as a result of this Focus Group.

What is a storyboard?

Each guest at your in-home Focus Group is given a personal and colorful workbook, we call a storyboard.

Storyboard Contents:
Getting to know you- demographics
5 question media survey- what are you reading, seeing or hearing?
5 question communications survey- how do you communicate and with whom?
Discussion topics.
Questions about specific advertising examples.

The storyboard leads you, and your guests through each 50 minute session.

At the end of each section, each respondent tallies a score based on their responses.

Each score reveals something interesting about the individual's consumer behavior.

Finally, the respondent tallies a total score for the whole workbook. You will help them discover the consumer profile that best represents them. It's fun, and surprising!

How you send the data:

After each Focus Group, go online to the IDI website, click on "send data" and follow each step. You will be entering each respondent's "total score" followed by how the scores break down by sections. Those scores help us put each bit of information into a spreadsheet database.

You payment is direct deposited within 24 hours. You are paid per "complete respondent"

Mail completed workbooks to IDI Headquarters for quality control, and further referencing.

***all information is completely anonymous and confidential. We do not even request contact information, though you may want to keep a guest book for your records and for future events.

<u>IDI Group FAQs</u>

What does IDI stand for?

IDI stands for the Image and the Description of the Image. So much of our success is based on the images we create. An image captures the imagination. It tells a story; and a story invites an audience.

How do I get compensated?

After your guests go home, simply email your data set to IDI headquarters. Your payment will automatically go into your direct deposit account within 24 hours.

Do my guests have to buy anything?

No. Absolutely not. In fact, we appreciate their input so much, we provide each participant with thank-you gifts adding up to over $20.00! Absolutely no sales involved.

What do I need to get started?

Simply register, and download the MANUAL. Give yourself plenty of time to go through it. Complete the certification process online, get your secure email, and get ready to research.

How does it work?

It's social marketing. You're great at it already. You enjoy talking to people, sharing information, and making personal connections.

Invite a group of guests to a friendly, no-sales Focus Group. We are only looking for their opinions, and constructive feedback about the household decisions that matter most. You lead discussions about consumer preferences, influences, and communications. Fill out fun surveys together. Review the latest advertisements. Takes notes, and enjoy.

What is the value in talking to people?

We believe that a conversation is the best way to learn. IDI Group represents the most intelligent consumer research, because we have talent like you, talking to real people, listening careful, and giving real value to their opinions.

What you need to begin:

A personal computer with internet.
Your secure email account
A printer, paper and ink (for printing fun surveys and handouts)
One digital voice recorder with USB available here:
www.bbbbb.com

Services:

IDI Consumer Research harvests and delivers advertising research to help your business communicate more effectively. Our innovative approach provides on-time, valuable feedback without compromising quality control or breaking the budget.

We combine the latest technology with the traditional values of a personal touch. We ask the community the right questions, listen attentively, and objectively pass those responses on to you.

The IDI Process:

First, we develop an understanding of your strengths and needs, and outline the research objectives.

Our field teams conduct friendly, in-person interviews with people in your community. We find out what forms of media are getting noticed, how people are communicating, and how they respond to your advertising.

Speech-to-text software and digital audio capture complete, honest, and real-life feedback. Then, we utilize a scientific approach to filter out the information you need, and deliver it within a format you can easily access
and share.

The Bottom Line:
Our unique methods allow us to provide an essential service that was previously unavailable to local businesses.

Success is providing a point of view that you have not yet considered. We look forward to showing you the most accurate picture of how community members respond to your communications.

The IDI Difference

"A conversation is the best way to learn. Have enough conversations and you will have an education."

Different is Better:

The problem for the research industry has been how to take the information that is contained within a respondent's *own words,* and turn that into easily organized data that you can access and share.

Previous methods could be time consuming, labor intensive, and unreliable. We developed a solution for our own urgent needs, and we are eager to share!

We efficiently capture data that was previously left on the cutting-room floor. We have pioneered a scientific method to take candid, valued conversations from local sources, and create one strong and powerful voice you can trust.

The IDI Commitment:
DIFFERENT PERSPECTIVES
HIGHLY VALUED DATA
QUALITY CONTROL
SCIENTIFIC APPROACHES
COST-EFFECTIVE METHODS

IDI data collection:
Our two-person field teams are friendly faces, who create an open environment where people feel comfortable to share.

The interviewer breaks the ice with specific questions about what kinds of media the respondent reads, sees, or hears; how the respondent communicates; with whom, and what do they share.

The interviewer displays an advertisement.

"Take a look at this ad. When you are ready, tell me how you feel about it. Take your time, and say anything you can think of."

The interviewer will note that the respondent provides information on
- the visual appeal of the ad
- the wording and content
- the respondent's interest in finding out more information through a website, phone call, or visit
- the respondent's likelihood to share or talk about the ad's information
- any comparisons or associations with other ads or businesses

The interviewer says only enough to maintain a pleasant atmosphere and keep the conversation going. The less the interviewer says, the less influence the interviewer has on the data. Each interview is transcribed with speech-to-text software for exceptional quality control.

The foundation of our analysis is the relationship between opinions and observations.

We provide information in the words of the consumer. We interview people in order to meet our research objectives. We organize that information. Then we present you with the highest value information in terms of exactly what you need to know.

We take multiple conversations and organize each statement, so that each statement is always followed by supporting statements. You can make a quick assessment, or dig as deep at you need to.

An opinion is an abstract statement that expresses an individual's like or dislike, preference or attitude. You can not visualize opinions, just as you cannot describe what thoughts look like.

An observation expresses an individual preference in terms of actions and activities, and sometimes situations. An observation is a statement that you could visualize or, theoretically, witness or see.

An opinion might be, "This ad is confusing."
An observation might be, "The text is difficult to read."
Both statements have a value, but it is important to distinguish between the two, and utilize both perspectives. Through comparison, we show stronger information, and create a system of checks and balances.

Visual Impact?

OPINIONS

OBSERVATIONS

other place."

"It's too small."
a. "I can't see anything."
b. "I need my glasses"

"I can't read the fine print."
a. "Where is the phone number? I can't find it."
b. "The picture covers everything up."

Text and Wording?

"It's boring."
a. "I can't even get through it."
b. "I'm lost!"

"Too many words."
a. "I don't understand this word."
c. "I'm not going to read all of this."

Does it create hunger for more info?

"I'd rather go to their website."
a. "I want one in red."
b. "I think I know where they are located. It's very nice."
c. "It's easier to call them and find out."

"I find out more online."
a. "I'll need more options."
b. "Here's their address"
c. "I'll remember the 1-800 number."

Share-able?

"My sister will love this."
a) "Someone told me about this once."
b) "I've always wanted to go! I'll ask my friend."

"The coupon is worth keeping. I'll cut it out."
a. "This is where my neighbor goes."
b. "I'll let the girls at work know."

Comparisons with other ads and businesses?

"It looks better than Versace."
a) "I used to love this at the other place."
b) "Did they have a better one of these in New York?"
c) "This is a worse deal than the

"I see these sorts of ads all the time."
a. "I don't pay attention to those sorts of places."
b. "The place I go now, does it cheaper."

IDI Group: consumer research

Thank you for your participation in our local media survey!

These ten quick questions will help local businesses better serve your needs!

1. What source(s) of local information do you consider the most reliable?
Newspapers (printed)
Newspapers (online)
Free newspapers
Websites
TV
Radio
direct mail
People you know
social media

2. What source(s) of local information do you pay attention to on a daily basis?
Newspapers (printed)
Newspapers (online)
Free newspapers
Websites
TV
Radio
direct mail
People you know
social media

3. How likely is it that you would share something with someone you know,
that you read, see, or hear from:

Newspapers (printed)	very likely 1	2	3	4	5	not likely
Newspapers (online)	very likely 1	2	3	4	5	not likely
Free newspapers	very likely 1	2	3	4	5	not likely
Websites	very likely 1	2	3	4	5	not likely
TV	very likely 1	2	3	4	5	not likely
Radio	very likely 1	2	3	4	5	not likely
direct mail	very likely 1	2	3	4	5	not likely
People you know	very likely 1	2	3	4	5	not likely
Social media	very likely 1	2	3	4	5	not likely

4. To get more information about a business, product, or service,
   are you MOST likely to:
A) visit a website
B) dial a phone number
C) visit in person
D) talk to someone you know

5. When you are shopping for something you NEED are you usually looking for:
A) the lowest price
B) the highest quality
C) the best value

6. When you are shopping for something you WANT are you usually looking for
A) the lowest price
B) the highest quality
C) the best value

7. If your preferred option is unavailable will you MOST likely buy:

A) the cheapest alternative
B) a similarly priced option
C) a better quality option
D) the option on sale

8. How many people, including yourself, live in your home? _____

9. About how many friends or family members, outside of your home, do you have at least weekly contact or communication?
A) 1-5
B) 6-10
C) 11-15
D) 16 or more

10. How do you usually contact or communicate with friends and family
     outside of your home? (circle any or all)
- Telephone (landline)
- Cell Phone
- Cellphone texting
- email
- chat online
- talk in person
- something in the mail
- social media (such as facebook, twitter)

Bonus: What are your top three websites that you visit on a weekly basis?

Consumer Categories

each categories has two questions to determine the respondent's archetype.

Media Exposure
online= 1
print= 2
TV and radio = 3

Communications
computer or print= 3
phone or texting =2
in person= 3

Shopping
lowest price= 1
highest quality = 2
best value = 3

Decision making
least expensive alternative= 1
similar value= 2
higher quality= 3

negotiation:
would you accept less right now =1
much more later =2
somewhat more somewhat sooner= 3

priorities
needs=1
wants= 2
investments (will you wait for better deal) =3

Shopping Archetypes:

In this example, imagine that you need laundry detergent.

1. When you are shopping around, are you usually looking for the option with:
    ⚓ lowest price = 1
    ⚓ highest quality = 2
    ⚓ best value = 3
2. When your preference is unavailable, would you consider the alternative with:
    ⚓ lowest price = 1
    ⚓ highest quality = 2
    ⚓ best value = 3
    Your score is represented by a co-ordinate pair (*preference/alternative*)

<u>Results:</u> there are nine consumer archetypes for the shopping category. Each archetype expresses a preference an an alternative. Each archetype is represented in the graph below. It would be easy to see how the data clusters.

```
3● ● ●
2● ● ●
1● ● ●
  1 2 3
```

Key to Archetypes:

(1, 1) always selects lowest price
(1, 2) usually selects lowest price, but would consider highest quality
(2, 1) usually highest quality, would consider lowest price
(1, 3) usually lowest price, would consider best value
(3, 1) usually best value, would consider lowest price
(2, 2) always highest quality
(3, 3) always best value
(2, 3) usually highest quality, would consider best value
(3, 2) usually best value, would consider highest quality

Two simple questions can show a lot of specific data.

⋏Correspondence:

IDI Group went live this morning. Very successful meeting yesterday. In a nut shell, businesses pay me to harvest information, refine information, and package information. I can do it better, quicker and cheaper, for a market that no else is accessing. I own the means of production, at last... and we always need more information.

Today... I shall rest. I'm having pancakes.

-x

I've been holed up, and very anti-social. I'm on this information kick. It's the new high. SNIFFFFFFF...formation.

I have overwhelmed this little ad agency with my own information. But they love every bit of it. She has the business, paperwork-y skills and set up... and she knows how to bill and swipe a credit card... How Lovely! She wants the verbal and creative skills.

I love advertising, because you can say whatever you want about yourself. It's the only form of free speech these days. Although, I witness and perpetuate the underbelly. Some things I observe at my employer make me nauseated. Information is power, and some use it for evil... I'm not even being dramatic for once. Do you think your cable provider really cares if you are satisfied with the quality of your picture service? That's not the info they use... disturbing...but not surprising.

In one sentence: "I harvest ad research that provides DIFFERENT and BETTER information, so that business can communicate a message more effectively." That's it. Sounds dry.... but you have to walk the walk sometimes.

Regardless, I have some sponsors for The Cinderella Shuffle. It's a smart idea disguised as something fluffy. Usually that's reversed. The event is inspired by the power of folk literature to carry a message across a culture for generations. But shhhh... don't tell anyone. I'm telling people they get FREE SHOES!

I'm a researcher in sheep's clothing... People act differently when they are being observed, right? Well, they don't know what exactly I am observing.

I don't really mention all of the deep stuff. It hurts sales. instead I say, "Hi, my name is X. Your Lobby is sooooo inviting! Is that granite?" It's work.

Phew! I'm exhausted... But that's what I do best!

I was feeling a little blue, Monday, so I started wheeling a dealing. that always makes me feel better. Sold some projects to a little ad agency, now I'm already needing to outsource. I love outsourcing. A better idea than the assembly line. let someone else do the chores.

I love working. It's really just about the attention. The world hasn't seen anything like me since Jackie Susann, and I... write happier endings!

It's an agency that works mostly with women. thank god. I developed a networking event I call, The Cinderella Swap! Use your imagination.

Hope things are well with you.

I wish I could give you a medal of honor... I admit I show my wildest, weirdest, worst at first, and then, I slowly open my eyes to see who is left. I am surprised and delighted every time you reply!

I don't even know who you are, you man of musicals! I must have clicked on your icon in a daydream. I click on lots of things, and usually nothing happens... I wish on lots of stars, and then I forget which stars I have already wished on... But, don't spoil it. You are a vagabond stranger on my time-traveling, up-and-down, merry-go-round in Maine!

I come on strong, I know, but I would rather know right away, if a stranger has any sort of courage at all.

But, I have scared people... and it always scares me more! Like a giant arriving in the middle of a fairytale village. Because, I am actually very small. Hardly more than Thumbelina!

But- in battles that matter, I am Napoleon!
In exile, I am Napoleon...
And, then, walking down the street, I am just as

easily Emily Dickenson. Crap!

But, once you write it down, you can never take it back. If you keep it secret, it is visible on your heart. So, we connect two words that have never known each other before, and we give a name to something that has never been named before! Words can only go forward... Hydrogen Jukebox!

But that's the point. I don't want to be a writer at all! I'm a good painter too, but it's dreadful to be a painter. My commodity is information! Of course it is! What would any reasonable person do with a block of gold? Oh god, I dream of a database of valued consumer information. And, my aspirations are truly virtuous. I want to give the power to the people, at least the reasonable people, or rather, someone who knows what to do with it.

What I do for work? God, talk about fudging.... shhh... asking freaking morons for their opinions on this and that is pretty useless. But what I learned is only that when the client is satisfied and paying the money, who cares....

anyway, what I do is I harvest information! Organize it, and interpret it. I want to say, My name is Mr. X, and I represent the largest continually updated database of consumer information! Trust in me, and we shall have better goods, faster services, a reduction of bullshit! Come to me, my huddled masses, my weak and geeky.... For the value of the individual, shall be the sum of his information! Every individual represents information. Even the homeless man owns the spot beneath his own to feet. He can hold a sign, and create a greater influence of information. He can stand in a better place and increase his value even more. There is hope for all!

I am as good with numbers as I am, I think, with words... I am working on a method to quantify an individual's worth based on the information they represent, and the influence they extend. That's fair. "Let my people go...." I am a capitalist, patriot... believe me if it is not cemented to the ground I can sell it. And I am a pacifist. I adore economic sanctions. Fighting wars with money and numbers. The USA defeated the soviet union, because we outspent them. "Each according to his information, each according to his level of communication...." Maybe that's a platform EVERYONE could agree on... cheers!

-X

www.ingramcontent.com/pod-product-compliance
Lightning Source LLC
Chambersburg PA
CBHW072030190526
45166CB00015B/1681